How to Get Started with CRO Workbook
Copyright © 2021 by Alexander Rådahl, RÅDAHL

ISBN 978-82-692592-6-1

Welcome

—

Thank you for getting my free Conversion Rate Optimization (CRO) workbook. I will do everything in my power and beyond to make this the best experience you have had and give you the tools to succeed in the future.

This workbook details how to start with CRO and the various methods that can be used to create a proper plan for your website and user experience. It will also give you many, good and bad, examples that can be used on real websites to tell you what works from the start and how to fix the things that are not. The biggest thing is that CRO takes time. You have to be patient and consistent with your strategies, otherwise they will not work.

ALEXANDER RÅDAHL

Alexander Rådahl

Alexander is a 26 years old Senior User Experience designer specialized in Customer Experience and Conversion Rate Optimization. He loves problem-solving, and as we all know, UX design is a process of solving problems. He likes to think of himself as a Design Detective, getting to the root cause of why people have certain feelings about your product. It's not just what you do; it's also what you don't do.

As an 11-year-old, Alexander already started programming his own websites and programs for the PC game *The Sims*. Working closely with Electronic Arts, he learned an incredible amount in development, design, marketing, and his website being the largest *The Sims* website in Norway.

As a skilled entrepreneur, Alexander has used his creativity and problem-solving skills in designing several products, both physical and digital. In the past few years alone, he has started a few companies, including an online store for home decor along with complex

solutions for larger ERP markets - all of which have allowed him to develop strong business acumen that can be applied across various industries. Whether it's creating brands or working on design projects from start to finish using new technologies like AR, you'll find Alexander's professional approach is always endearing and compelling.

Alexander is passionate about UX design, and he sees it as a process of problem-solving. The core for any conversion optimization campaign is to understand the user's needs, desires, behaviors, motivations, etc., and tap into the psychological part of the user.

What is UX?

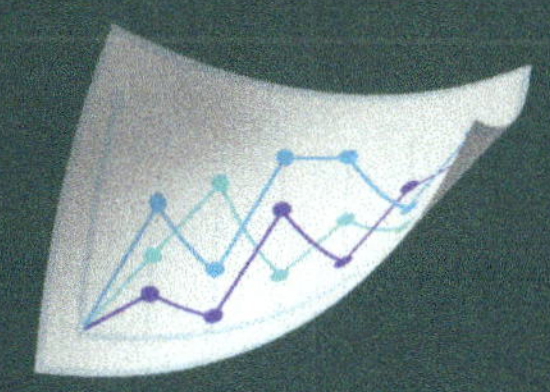

User Experience, or UX, design is the practice of understanding users, their needs, and their goals to create a human-centric interface. A user interface should be easy to understand and give the information in a clear and simple way to the user. Information should be readable and understandable, without having to decipher it. Effective UX design can help save money by avoiding costly mistakes in development by carrying out usability tests early on.

UX design has many advantages, including its ability to increase productivity, expand markets, improve customer satisfaction, and reduce development costs. UX design has become an integral part of a company's marketing strategy. The aim is to give the user the best possible experience when making a purchase or using your website, so that they are more likely to take action.

It is important that UX designers know how people use their products and services to create a seamless UX design. An outstanding UX designer should be able to create a user experience that meets the needs of the company and visually appeals to its audience.

What is CRO?

Conversion rate optimization (CRO) is the process of increasing website conversion through scientific methods. CRO helps improve customer satisfaction, increase a company's revenues, and save development costs by carrying out usability tests early in the process. CRO is important because it makes websites more accessible to users and easier to navigate, which leads to higher user satisfaction and the likelihood that they will buy from your business.

CRO can vary depending on what the owner of the website wants to achieve. It is important to understand how visitors visit your website and which elements of the site make them stop visiting it. CRO involves using data analysis tools like Google Analytics to find the changes that need to be made to convert the website to its customers. CRO is a continuous process that involves trial and error, testing various methods and reading customer feedback to find the one that works best for you.

All websites can benefit from CRO because it improves user satisfaction and saves development costs by carrying out usability tests early. The aim is to create an effective, user-centric website that offers your customers a better experience. CRO can vary according to what you want to achieve.

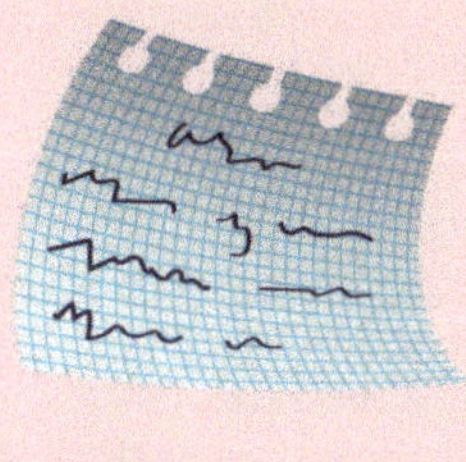

Contents of this workbook

Chapter 04: Three types of CRO strategies — 41

Chapter 05: The way forward with CRO and UX — 53

Chapter 06: More resources for CRO and UX — 57

Introduction to Self-Assessment & Goals

Before we start the workbook, it is important that you or your team understand your current knowledge of conversion rate optimization (CRO) and UX design. I have created a self-assessment that you can take. This part should not be rushed, and you should only answer it on the basis of your current knowledge (no use of Google!). If you're a team, you can do it together or even print out more versions so that everyone can take it alone and compare the results.

I have also included some goals you can set yourself or your team after taking the quiz, as well as some resources below that will help you better understand CRO and UX design. If you're completely new to this, check out everything I'm proposing in this book.

Depending on how you answer the quiz, some of these resources will be more relevant than others - which is perfect if you are still just starting optimizing your site! If your results range from 10-30 points, check out the accompanying book of this workbook "Winning The Game with UX Design and CRO" for more in-depth beginner content.

Self-Assessment

01. How familiar are you with the term Conversion Rate optimization?

1 2 3 4 5 6 7 8 9 10

02. How important is bounce rate when it comes to CRO?

1 2 3 4 5 6 7 8 9 10

03. How familiar are you with A/B testing?

1 2 3 4 5 6 7 8 9 10

04. How comfortable are you with tools like Google Analytics and Hotjar?

1 2 3 4 5 6 7 8 9 10

05. How well can data analysis tools be used to identify conversion rates?

1 2 3 4 5 6 7 8 9 10

06. In your opinion, how much does SEO matter in CRO?

1 2 3 4 5 6 7 8 9 10

07. How complex is it to learn to use data analysis tools, in your opinion?

1 2 3 4 5 6 7 8 9 10

08. How much difference can CRO make to your business?

1 2 3 4 5 6 7 8 9 10

09. In your opinion, how much does social media presence help in CRO?

1 2 3 4 5 6 7 8 9 10

10. How important is email marketing for conversion rates?

1 2 3 4 5 6 7 8 9 10

What's your score?

10-30 You're a beginner in CRO, congratulations! You have come to the right place. This book will get you off the ground and understand what the methods of CRO.

31-60 You know some of the methods for CRO and UX, but could use a little more knowledge in this field. You need to fill in any gaps, so you can be an expert!

61-100 You're not only an expert, it looks like you know everything! This book would be a great way to make sure your future work is flawless.

Setting Your Goals

The first step is to determine where you want to go

01. What do you want to achieve strategically with CRO?

02. What do you want to achieve financially with CRO?

03. What do you hope to get help with in this workbook?

04. What are you currently struggling with in CRO?

05. What are your priorities in achieving your goals in CRO?

Getting Started

Your intetions going forward

I am going to:

ex. build a 6 figure eCommerce business in the next two years.

What limitations do I have to overcome to achieve this:

ex. I don't know how to get started with building it or improve CRO.

What steps do I have to take to get started:

ex. start learning about CRO and web development.

What tools do I need to get started:

ex. just my computer.

Why am I doing this:

ex. I want to become a expert in my field.

I am greatful for:

ex. the opportunity to pursuse my dream.

01

How to get started with CRO

In this chapter, I will guide you through the basics of conversion rate optimization. You will learn how to analyze your website and understand what is important for a high conversion rate and how to improve it.

Getting started

There are many ways to get started with CRO as a designer or even business owner. You can take courses on the subject, start reading about it online (like you do now!), or even talk to a CRO expert.

I also recommend you have your website reviewed by an expert in CRO, so that they can give you recommendations and tips for improvement. However, I am aiming for yours being able to do it yourself after you have finished this workbook.

It's never been easier to get started with CRO! There are many tools and resources that it can be difficult to know where to start. In this chapter, I will give you a breakdown of the basics: How do I conduct A / B tests, how do I measure my conversion rates, what tools are available to me, etc.

Google Analytics

Many designers now use Google Analytics to help them understand their customer journey.

Although it is crucial to understand the basics - what page people land on, how they navigate through your website - you can get a much better understanding of conversion rates by looking at some more specific data points within Google Analytics. The tool is installed on 29 million websites.

Google Analytics is a free web analytics tool that can be used to track traffic patterns, traffic sources, and goal conversion rates in real time. You can also track common metrics, including sessions and sessions, and identify where visitors leave or which web pages have high bounce rates.

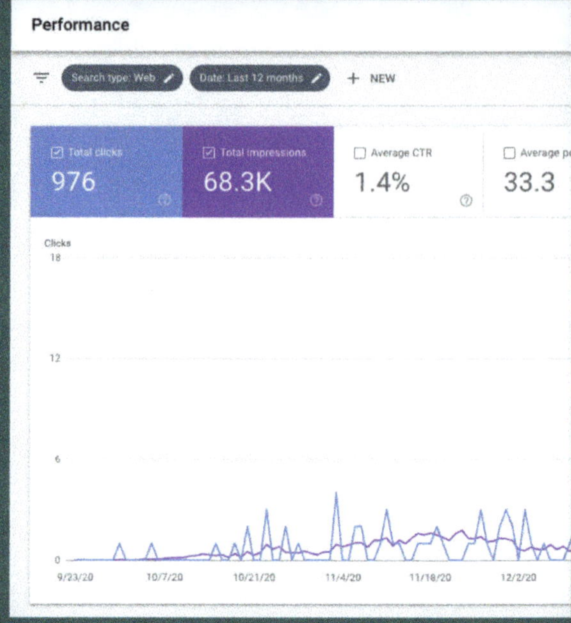

We are all familiar with the Google search engine; what you might not know is it also has a tool for website publishers called the Google Search Console!

It's an SEO (Search Engine Optimization) service that helps site owners understand how their site appears to crawlers or bots on major search engines like Google, Yahoo!, Bing, AOL, etc. This information will help you identify any crawling errors, so they can be fixed immediately.

It goes without saying - I would recommend using Google Search Console daily when looking at your traffic source stats in Google Analytics.

Google Search Console

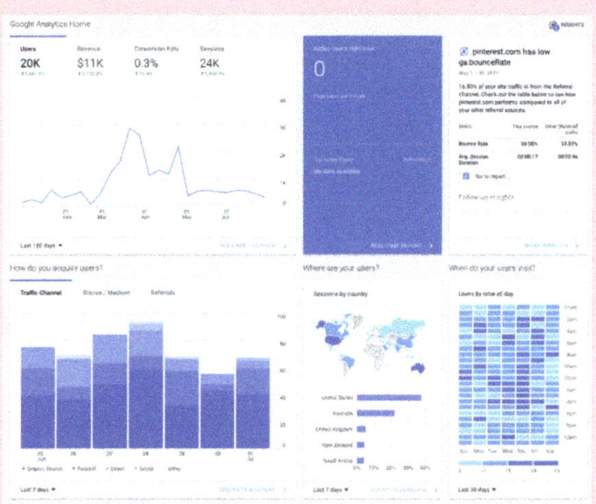

GTMetrix

GTMetrix is a free web-based tool to measure how fast your site loads.

The GTMetrix team has developed a proprietary algorithm that measures the load time of every single request on your website and provides you with a complete page speed rating, information about individual requests and suggestions for improvements.

Speed is one key factor in UX: it affects conversion rates by up to 11%. You also have no control over third party providers like social media widgets or ads if they use their own high capacity servers rather than yours. A/B testing can help determine which provider works better, so there's less guesswork involved when making these decisions! GTmetric helps identify what may be slowing down different parts of your websites - including images, scripts and host names. GTMetrix is a free UX tool that can help you measure how fast your site loads and where to start with optimizations for CRO!

GTMetrix is a UX tool that can help you measure how quickly your site loads and where to start with optimizations for CRO!

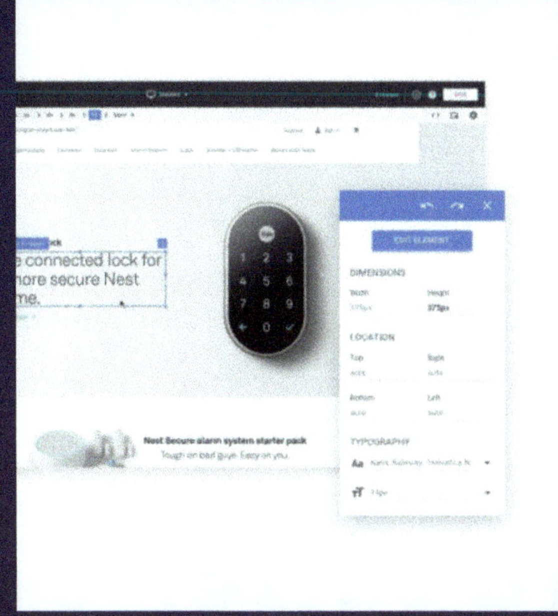

Google Optimize is a free, powerful web analytics tool that can be used to optimize your conversion rates on both mobile and desktop devices.

It provides you with insights into what people are doing on your site and what steps they take to convert. It also allows UX professionals to test different pages for an increased chance of converting visitors into customers or leads - Google Optimize lets you change content without making code changes!

Information that is collected from this software will help companies make data-driven decisions and thus achieve their goals faster than ever!

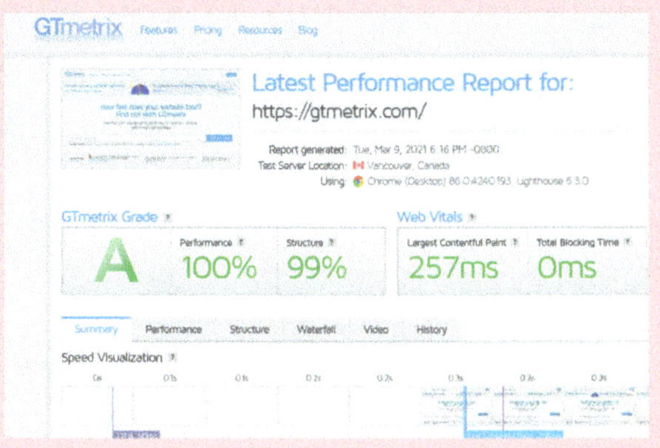

Google Optimize

Heap Analytics

Heap Analytics is a powerful tool that helps you understand who your customers are and what they do on your site.

It helps you quickly identify problems and measure performance in order to make data-driven decisions about UX design in real time.

With Heap Analytics, you can better understand what your users are doing on your site by tracking their activity and engagement in real time through heat maps, scroll maps, click maps, and form analyses. You could use this information to quickly identify problems on your site, including broken links or unclear CTAs (calls-to-action).

Heap also offers A / B testing functionality, where you can test two versions of content to determine which version works better for conversions without manually implementing the changes.

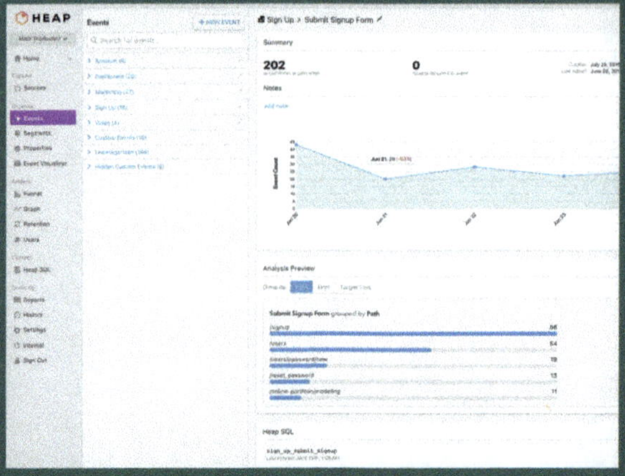

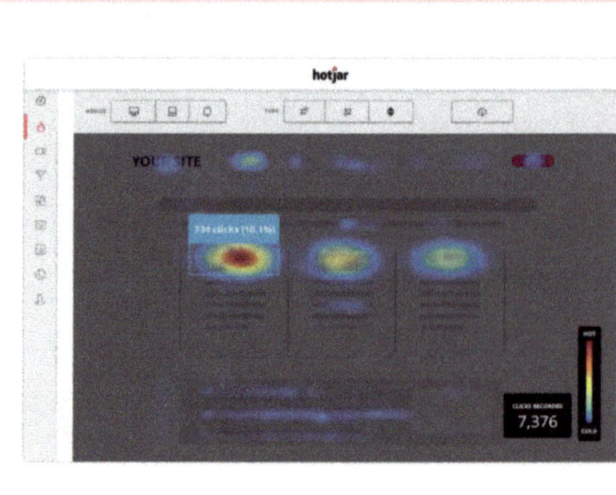

Hotjar is a UX and CRO tool that helps you understand how your users interact with your website.

You can visualize what they are doing on the site, watch videos of them using it, ask questions about their experiences with it, and get into the real stoppers to understand why people are not turning to buyers.

Hotjar also offers A / B testing functions, where you can test two versions of content against each other to see which one works better for conversions without manually implementing the changes. There is also functionality to directly view recorded sessions of users.

Hotjar's UX and CRO features are particularly useful for businesses where they want to understand how users experience their site. With Hotjar, you can make UX improvements on your website without waiting for the next design project or hiring a UX agency. I always use this tool when I start a project to ensure that I have a full picture of the current user experience.

Hotjar

Optimizely

Optimizely is a design optimization platform that allows designers to create and test variations in their digital designs.

It provides both qualitative data from user surveys and quantitative data, such as conversion rates. Some big names have used the tool, including Airbnb, Walmart, and Target.

Optimizing your website is not a one size fits all task. What works for one company may not work for another. Still, luckily there are many

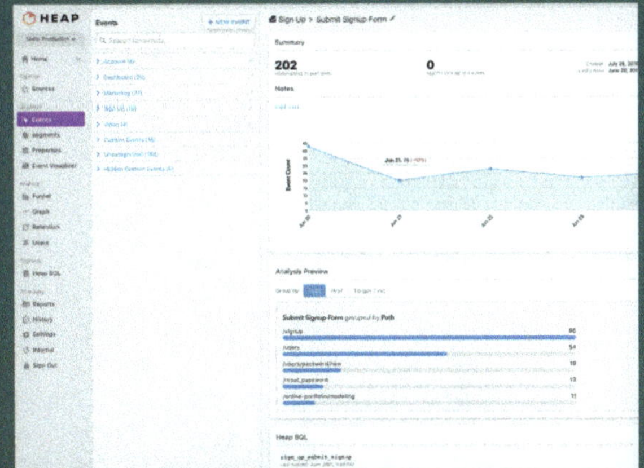

great tools out there to help you make the best decision about which optimization strategy-will get you the most results in your particular industry.
Check out this list of CRO tools and see what might be right for you!

Key Takeaways

UX and CRO are important for companies of all sizes, but the UX professionals at GTMetrics are here to help you make decisions with more confidence.

If you're looking to increase conversions without making code changes, Google Optimizely is an excellent option. Using any of these tools will ensure you have a head start in the game and can close more sales.

02

The first steps in a CRO campaign

CRO campaigns are about one thing: conversion.
Learn how to get started and work with the tools I use
everyday as a CRO expert.

The first steps in a successful CRO campaign

CRO campaigns are about one thing: conversion. If your goal is to increase conversions, you must take a step-by-step approach that will lead you down the path to CRO success.

Often it starts with looking at the data you have already collected through various tools and insights within your team or organization. This could be Google Analytics, talking to the sales or marketing department, or directly with previous buyers.

It is important to do research and better understand your customers before you start trying CRO strategies. What are their needs, what do they do now? How do we make them happier with our products or services? You can use the questions on the right side to help you get these answers.

Once you have discovered these findings, it will be much easier to create CRO campaigns that meet your specific needs.

One interesting finding was, that when I asked these questions to myself, our users, and the team, that many people believed the checkout process was too complicated, and it would be better if they could speak directly to a sales representative who could help them. The data you collect allows you to know more about what happens in your product. It is worthwhile to take some time to do this basic research before you start!

After researching what customers need, you should start thinking about solutions to the problems. Often it can help to create different personas or user stories for the problems you have discovered. This will give you a better understanding of the customer and give us different solutions.

By setting up a chat bot at the right time for one eCommerce client I was able to increase their conversion rates by 5%.

Why are they not converting?

Find out why they don't convert by asking these questions

Where is the bottle neck?

What are the UX issues?

Do they know about all of our features and benefits?

Are we targeting the right people with ads or offers that do not appeal to them?

The right CRO strategy can save you time

With the rise of digital marketing, it has become easier for companies to compete and have their voice heard. Not all companies however, take advantage of this opportunity. Some companies still make mistakes that can easily be avoided with a little bit of planning.

01

Not understanding what your goals are for your campaign.

02

Thinking about CRO as an isolated project rather than part of a larger plan.

03

Not testing different types of ads in different channels.

The rise in digital marketing has given companies the opportunity to compete. However, not every company even takes advantage of this opportunity and still makes mistakes that can easily be avoided with a little planning. Digital marketers have realized how important CRO is for their success and are looking at it as an integral part of any campaign rather than just another project on the list.

The importance of A/B testing

Do you ever feel your work is not good enough? Are you questioning how well people will react to it in the market and wondering if all this time and effort is simply a waste, or worse, a complete failure? Well, there's a way to find out: A / B testing! We have already touched a little bit on A / B testing, but I wanted to go a little more in detail here and how it can be used in a successful CRO campaign.

Just a refresher on what A/B testing looks like:
A/B testing is a process that involves randomly showing two (or more) different designs to your audience and seeing which one performs better. This can be done on landing pages, social media posts, or any other type of marketing material.

In an A/B test, when the user lands on a page or clicks through to it from social media, you randomize which design is shown. Once they've seen both designs and completed an action (ex: clicked "buy"), you randomly assign them again. This continues until there are enough people who have viewed each variation of the experiment for you to see what performs better with your audience - this might be whichever version gets more purchases or any converting factor that is important for your business. The process can be repeated over and over again for different versions of your website or marketing material so that you know what will work best with your customers.

We often see that working with A/B testing can significantly increase the conversion rate as you use real-life proof of what actually is shown to the user, not just a subjective meaning.

A/B testing examples

I worked with a fashion e-commerce customer who wanted to know which pop-up for their newsletter would increase their conversion rate. They had some thoughts on design and incentive. One was a small gift with the first order, the second was a 10% discount, and the third was a combination of the two.

I then decided to create an A/B test with their email marketing software to compare it, and we could observe a clear trend:

- Gift only: Converted 2% of the time
- Discount only: 0.62% conversion rate
- Combination: 8% conversion rate

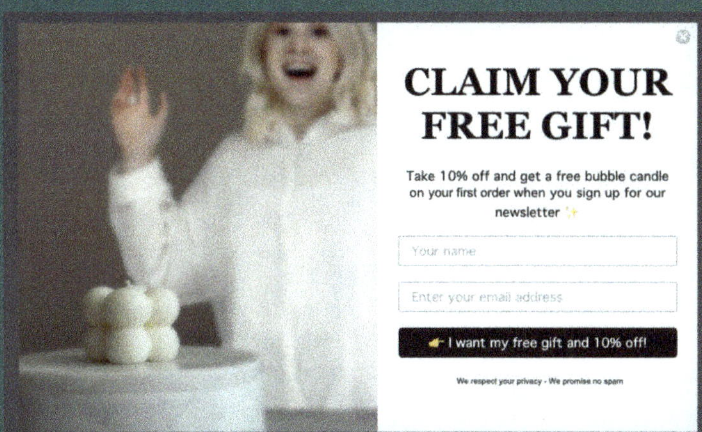

We thought it would convert better with the gift and discount, but we were also afraid that might be too much information to give at once. We had no idea how dramatically different our conversion rate could have been!

Key Takeaways

The first step in CRO is to identify the desired conversion state. What are you trying to convert? It could be a purchase, an e-mail registration, or any other type of action that benefits the company's business goals.

Once this is determined, you would have to think about what steps could help achieve this, and how these changes can affect customer behavior during their visit to the site and drive them toward those crucial final touches, such as adding items to shopping carts or completing the checkout process.

This requires a mindset of CRO thinking when planning and designing the service, and we have touched on some of them in this chapter.

The Cheat Sheet

This list will make your life easier

User: A person who views the site or enters your website.

Conversion: The act of turning a visitor into a customer by applying a call to action, like filling out a form, downloading/purchasing something online, etc.

Analytics: Analysis of data generated from website traffic and user interactions with the site in order to measure their effectiveness.

A/B testing: A method of optimizing conversion rates in which different variations are created and tested against each other to see which one works better.

CRO process: The process of using various techniques/strategies to improve conversion rates.

Funnel: The set of steps a user takes to complete an action. Such as signing up or completing a purchase.

Value proposition: The specific reason why someone should choose to do business with you over another company.

Bounce rate: The percentage of visits in which the user views only one page on your site and then leaves without interaction.

Other notes:

03

Get into the work with CRO!

In this chapter, we will dive even deeper into how to use CRO in your next project with exercices that you should do to get started!

Go to Market

Define your goals for the project

When you work on a new project for yourself or a client, it's important to understand all the different aspects of your project and the goal you have in mind.

Action List

My priorites for the next month

Goal no. One

Deadline:

Outcome I want to achieve:

Why this is important:

Steps I have to take:

Goal no. Two

Deadline:

Outcome I want to achieve:

Why this is important:

Steps I have to take:

Goal no. Three

Deadline:

Outcome I want to achieve:

Why this is important:

Steps I have to take:

Get into it with the action list

By using the CRO Action List I have created (on the previous page), you will be able to define some of the future goals you want to achieve with CRO. It is critical that you understand precisely why you are doing an action and what the desired result is, before you start any sort of CRO campaign or UX improvement, otherwise you do not know why you are doing it, for whom you are doing it, or how you measure the results.

After filling in the action list, I want you to go more in detail about each of the goals you have defined, with the worksheets for goal definition and the action matrix I have created - you will finde them on the next pages. This will even further flesh out your goals and challenge you in your thoughts.

So let's get started! And remember: have fun with this!

Goal No. One

Write it down, plan it, and get it done

The Goal

The Strategy

Steps to Take

-
-
-
-
-
-
-

Notes

The Action Matrix

Write it down and work on it

My goal is:

Goal No. Two

Write it down, plan it, and get it done

The Goal

The Strategy

Steps to Take

-
-
-
-
-
-
-

Notes

The Action Matrix

Write it down and work on it

Goal No. Three

Write it down, plan it, and get it done

The Goal

The Strategy

Steps to Take

-
-
-
-
-
-
-

Notes

The Action Matrix

Write it down and work on it

Introduction to the art of Personas

Personas are an important part of user experience design and CRO. They help you better understand your user's goals, needs, motivations, frustrations, and desires, so you can create a website or app that meets their expectations. In this part of the workbook, I will explore the importance of personas in both UX design and CRO, and give you some tasks to do to get the feeling of working with personas.

01. Personas help UX designers by giving insights into the perspective of users they may not have considered before.

02. Personas give designers information about what motivates people to use certain features on websites.

03. Personas provide valuable insights into how customers want their content delivered - like video versus text.

04. Personas allows us to develop a stronger message to get the user "hooked" and increase the conversion rate.

The personas help you better understand the goals, needs, motivations, frustrations, and desires of your users, so you can create a website or app that meets their expectations. There are a few tasks you should do to get the feeling of working with personas. You need to know your persona's goal and divide it into different contexts. After that, think about what people want to achieve in these situations. For example, "I want to learn more about my health" may mean they need to find information about drugs and treatments for diseases and illnesses. This information could be best made through video, because videos allow viewers to see their health professionals talk about their condition in detail - something text or articles cannot offer.

Personas are like your representative users: they can be stereotypical, but their traits come from real people you have spoken to and learned about. The more research you do, the better you will get. So start by researching a customer persona per week for the next five weeks. Ideally, you should talk to customers through interviews or surveys, and ask them engaging and open questions about their experiences with your site or app. On the next page, I have provided several printed templates that you can practice and make personas.

Persona Worksheet

Write down who your persona is to get a clear picture of who you're designing for

Who am I?

Perona name:

Age:

Gender:

Occupation:

Location:

Highest level of education:

Annual income:

My interests

My personality

Goals and motivations

Reasons to engage

Reasons not to engage

01.

02.

03.

01.

02.

03.

Persona Worksheet

Write down who your persona is to get a clear picture of who you're designing for

Perona name:

Age:

Gender:

Occupation:

Location:

Highest level of education:

Annual income:

Who am I?

My interests

My personality

Goals and motivations

Reasons to engage	Reasons not to engage
01.	01.
02.	02.
03.	03.

Persona Worksheet

Write down who your persona is to get a clear picture of who you're designing for

Perona name:

Age:

Gender:

Occupation:

Location:

Highest level of education:

Annual income:

Who am I?

My interests

My personality

Goals and motivations

Reasons to engage

01.

02.

03.

Reasons not to engage

01.

02.

03.

Persona Worksheet

Write down who your persona is to get a clear picture of who you're designing for

Perona name:

Age:

Gender:

Occupation:

Location:

Highest level of education:

Annual income:

Who am I?

My interests

My personality

Goals and motivations

Reasons to engage	Reasons not to engage
01.	01.
02.	02.
03.	03.

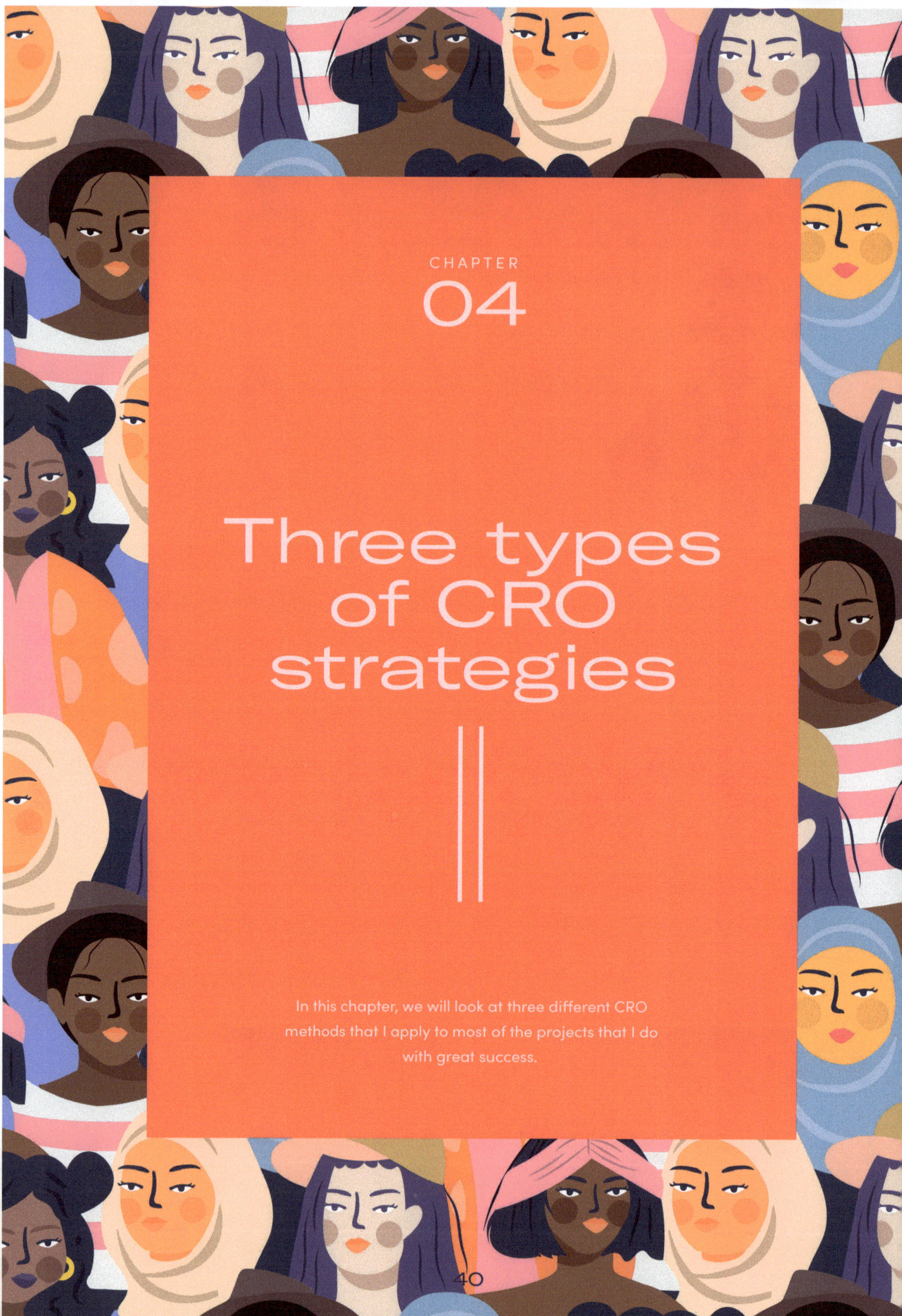

CHAPTER
04

Three types
of CRO
strategies

In this chapter, we will look at three different CRO
methods that I apply to most of the projects that I do
with great success.

The three types of CRO strategies

Does your design process lead you in the right direction? How can you know whether or not your design is successful?

With CRO and UX design, there are endless possibilities. Just like in any new field in its infancy phase, there is still so much to explore and research to discover. For a young industry space with unlimited innovation potential, I encourage you to be boundary pushers who lead this pioneering profession!

In my CRO strategies, there are three types: UX optimization, A / B testing, and funnel analysis. Each of them has its own advantages and disadvantages, so it is important to choose the one that best suits you and your business needs. Let's look at it more closely!

The three types of CRO strategies

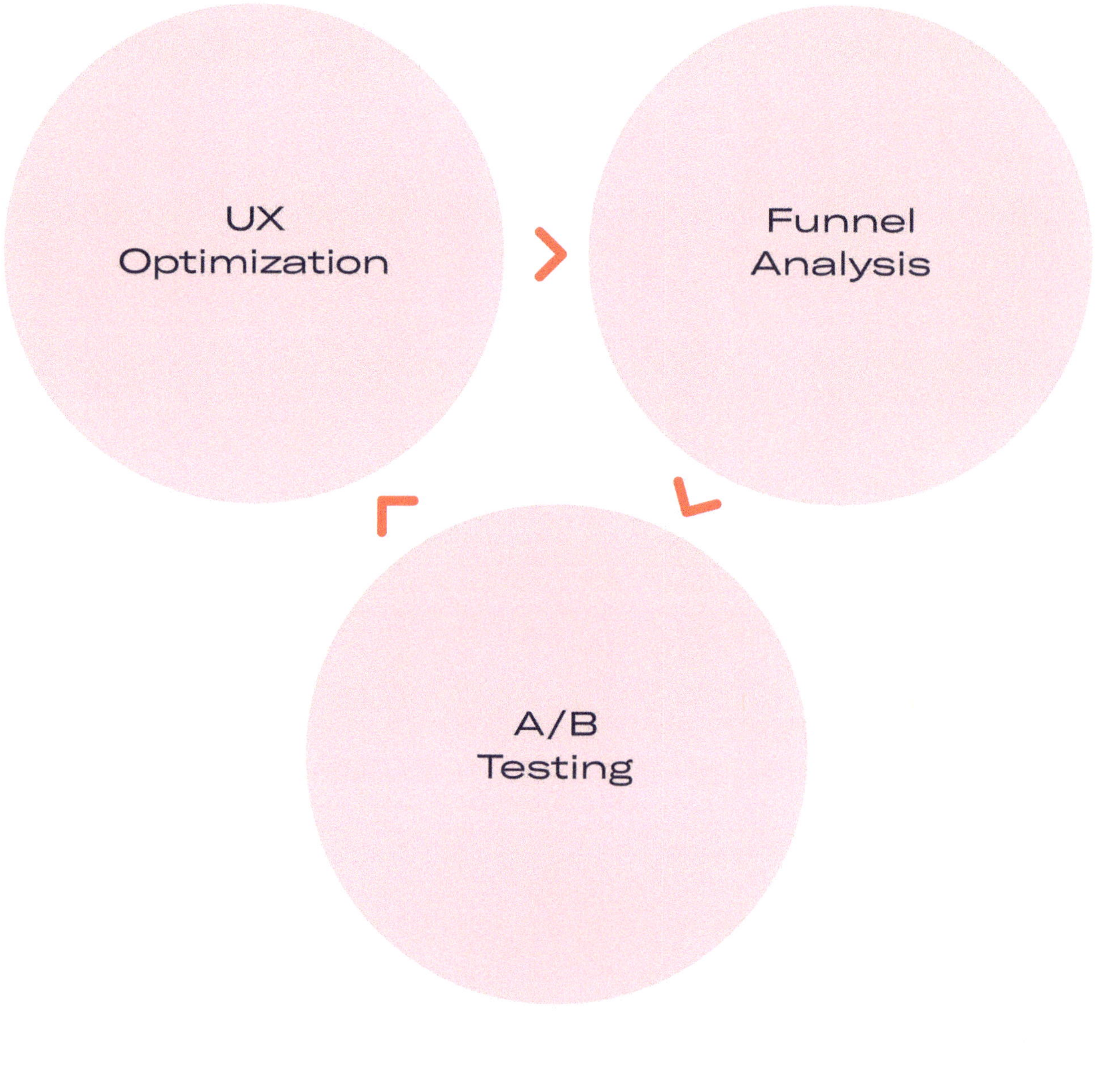

The three types of CRO strategies

Does your design process lead you in the right direction? How can I know whether or not my design is successful?
With CRO and UX design, there are endless possibilities. Just like in any new field in its infancy phase, there is still so much to explore and research to discover

UX
Optimization

The term UX optimization is a bit of an oxymoron, so we have to break it down. The two words combined can be understood as "the process of making something more user-friendly or efficient," which is somewhat true, but the word has no official definition, so we should look a little more into it.

When it comes to making something more user-friendly, there are many ways to do this. You could make the layout less cluttered or colorful, so people know where they are going and what they need from the website. If someone is looking for information on how many calories are needed per day, an important button should be at the eye level, rather than way down a page with tons of other buttons - which will help them get their answer faster. The point is when we think about UX optimization, we must consider not only "user experience," but also the impact that our decisions might have on "efficiency."

You also need to remember it is not just about improving the user experience, but also to understand how people will use your product. It is important to remember that UX optimization is not a one-off thing. You have to analyze and change your design to keep it relevant constantly.

Funnel analysis

Success is the best way to measure what you do right. If you do not measure success, how do you know if your efforts are worth it? The tricky part is to figure out which metrics are most important for your business.

Here are some questions to ask yourself when deciding what matters:

1. What does my audience care about?
2. How do I want them to feel?
3. What do they need?
4. How do I want them to behave?
5. What am I trying to achieve with my UX design or CRO efforts?

The goal of a UX designer is not only to solve the problem, but also to create something people like. It is important for you as a UX designer to know what your users care about and how they will feel when they interact with them. Once you understand this, you can start designing to achieve those goals. Your focus should be on finding out who your target audience is and figuring out which metrics are most valuable for measuring success – regardless of conversion rates or engagement levels.

This often begins with the funnel analysis, and what is a funnel you might ask? A funnel is a process in which a person takes one action and then moves on to the next. This could be the flow of a user from landing on the page until he buys a product or registers for a service. The UX designer's goal with this type of analysis is to find out where users drop off at certain points in the process.

The conversion rate can also be considered a way for UX designers to measure the success of the funnel. How to measure the success of the efforts in UX and CRO depends heavily on the type of business you run or work for.
More often than not, certain tools are used to make this type of analysis. I mentioned some of them earlier in the book, and I will also touch them a little more later.

Conversion rates can be considered for UX designers to measure success depending on the type of business you run or work in – more likely, certain tools are used for this type of analysis.

A/B Testing

In its simplest form, A/B testing is a technique for comparing two versions of a webpage or application to determine which version works better.

In UX, A/B tests are often used to find out which design variation of a website works better. Common goals in UX are to maximize conversion rates and minimize the time spent on individual tasks, such as browsing through products or navigating categories.

A/B tests can be used at various stages of the process and help a UX designer determine which direction he should take. UX designers can use A/B tests to find out which UX design patterns are more popular and should therefore be implemented more often.
If we look at CRO and A/B tests, it is the perfect tool to determine the most optimized design and funnel flow for a higher conversion rate.

CRO & UX Venn Diagram

CRO Side:

01. Adequate speed

02. Optimized for conversions

03. Great content

The Overlap Area

UX Side:

01. Optimal usability

02. Great user experience

03. Thoughtful patterns

CRO Side

The CRO is about creating an experience and story that leads the user to take action, such as purchasing a product or signing up for membership.

UX Side

The UX is about creating an attractive user experience that makes the user feel comfortable and understand what is happening on the site you are currently browsing.

The Overlap Area

It is important to understand that UX and CRO go hand in hand. You will not get a high conversion without a great user experience, and you will not get a satisfactory conversion rate with only a compelling user experience. The biggest mistake I made in my start-up was to focus too much on the user experience and forget the conversion rate and how to get more customers. The result? Our site revenue was very low and I decided to close the site and focus on learning CRO.

The CRO Funnel Diagram

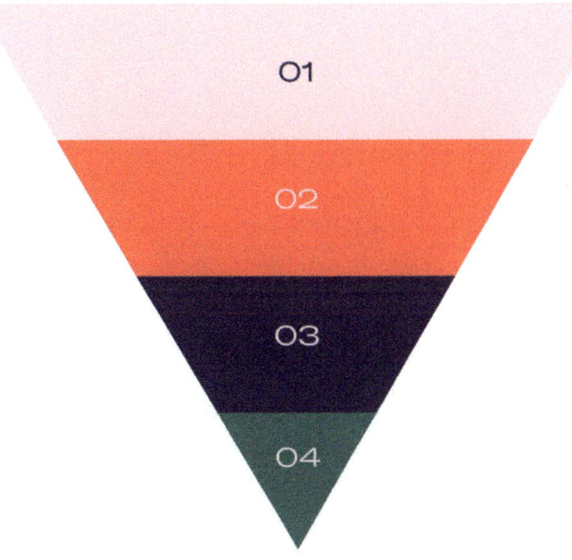

01. Awareness ❯ 02. Interest ❯ 03. Consideration ❯ 04. Conversion

01

Awareness

The awareness phase is the point at which a potential customer becomes aware they might need your product. it's also the first contact with your business, so if you want to convert them into a customer, you must stand out as much as possible from your competitors.

02

Interest

Interest is the second phase of the CRO funnel and it's about getting your customers to know more about you. At this stage, you should aim to be as informative as possible without bombarding your customers with too much information.

03

Consideration

The consideration phase of the CRO funnel is to inform your customers and persuade them to buy your product or service. You should not push buyers to make a decision, but ensure they are informed as much as possible to make the best decision for their needs.

04

Conversion

The conversion phase is when you get your customer to act and buy. This is, of course, the ultimate goal for each funnel, and as such it must focus on the call to action. What do you want the customer to do? Buy? Sign up for updates? All of this can be different parts of the conversion phase in CRO.

CRO Checklist

Use this checklist for every project to see if you have implemented the
core methods of CRO

01. Define the purpose of the project

It is important to understand why you are doing what you are doing, and it is even more
important to understand what your goals are for the project.

02. Create clear conversion goals

As mentioned in the previous point, the key to any CRO project is to establish goals and
methods for measuring success. Therefore, come up with 2-3 key factors for success.

03. Write out your expectations

Based on the two above, create a clear vision for the project you want to start, and create
an outline of how your goals are aligned with it.

04. Determine required resources

Create an overview of the resources you need to achieve your goals. This could be Heap.io
or other tools, such as Adobe Xd.

05. Choose your approach and research best practices

You should now have a clear path to what approach you want to take. Write it down and
do your research.

06. Draft a plan with steps on what needs to be done

The plan should include who will do it, when and what resources they will need to fulfill
their task. Here is a perfect time to use Action Priority Matrix.

07. Validate your plan with stakeholders

It is important to validate what you have just done, which can be done with a stakeholder,
colleague, friends and family. It's up to you! If you need more tasks, use the next sheet.

08. Implement!

The last, but perhaps the most important step, is to implement your plan and keep an eye
on the analytics tool to verify whether it works and tweak it along the way.

Checklist Worksheet

Prioritize and write down what you feel is important for your next CRO project

01.

02.

03.

04.

05.

06.

07.

08.

09.

10.

11.

12.

13.

14.

15.

Other:

Action Priority Matrix

Determine what you should do and in what order

High Impact

Low Impact

Quick Wins

Major Projects

Filler Tasks

Thankless Tasks

Low Effort

High Effort

My Notes:

Winning The Game with UX Design & CRO!

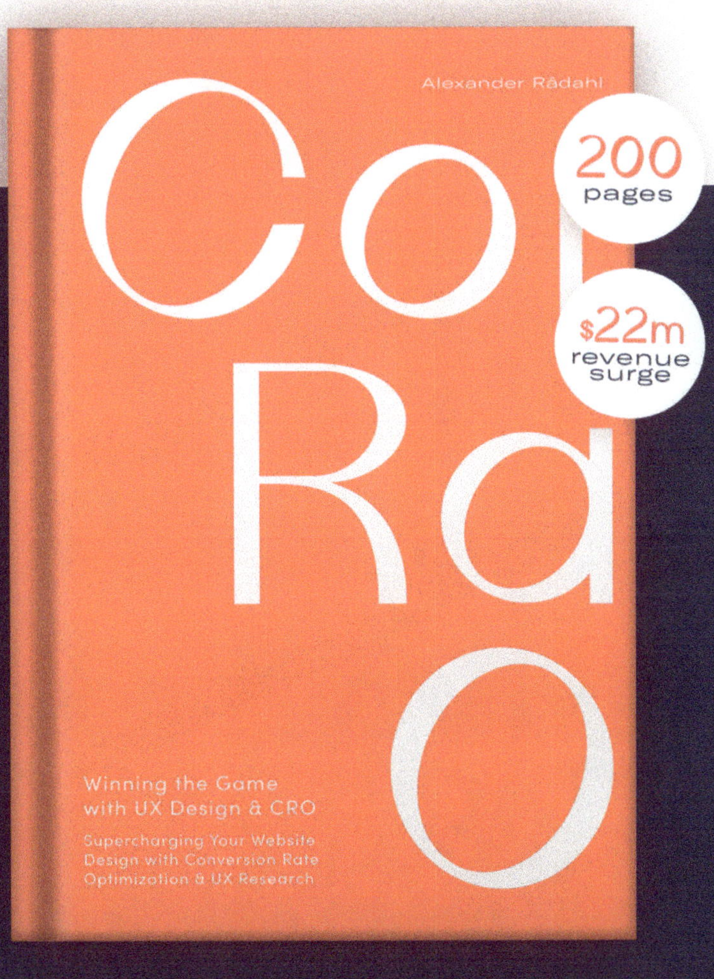

Learn how I helped a client with a 15% increase in their conversion rates - that means a surge of $22 million dollars for their business!

Knowledgeable and insightful CRO & UX content. Whether you want to start experimenting or need some inspiration for your next project, this book has something for everyone.

Learn how to create high performing landing pages CRO & UX. With our step-by-step guide, you'll be able to take any idea and turn it into a high performing website with little effort.

Rock your CRO & UX skills! You don't have to worry about setting up a complicated system or hiring a consultant – this book has everything you need!

Get the Book

The way forward with CRO and UX

How do you move forward from this book and apply it to your daily working life?

The Next Steps Forward

01
Get familiar with CRO

Get to know what CRO is and how you can use it in your daily work as a UX designer or marketer.

02
Practise CRO

By working yourself through this book and applying what you learn here you will have a headstart to the game of CRO.

03
Read more about CRO

By diving deeper and learning more about CRO and the practise of UX design, you will be able to add even more tools to your belt for how to increase conversions.

04
Apply your learnings

By using these methods and learnings in your proejcts you will get familiar with them and they will become a natural part of your workflow.

05
Teach others

Help someone else who wants to get started in CRO by teaching them the methods and functions behind it, in this way you will enfore the learning for yourself too!

06
Experiment

Try out new methods and find your own way by experimenting with A/B testing and other tools you will learn in the book "Winning The Game with UX Design & CRO".

Do the 30-day challenge!

We have created a 30-day CRO challenge for readers like you to help you get ahead of the curve. The aim is to help you improve your conversion rates and build your expert skills in CRO, so you can be more effective in your work.

I know that most people do not have time to take on a new skill like this during their busy day, but since it's only a 30 days challenge, we think it will be worth it for many of you.

It is easy to read about a new skill and admire the examples, but a skill will only improve if you practice it yourself. And one of the best ways to practice is to set time on your calendar as a reminder and force yourself to follow.

So let's do it together!

30 Day Challenge

Challenge yourself to be a better CRO expert and UX designer

01 Calculate current conversion rate	**02** Identify one way to improve bounce rate	**03** Analyze three competitors	**04** Set your conversion goals	**05** Find your value proposition	**06** Set up Google Analytics
07 Set up Hotjar	**08** Ask current customers questions	**09** Try something new	**10** Run a survey	**11** Create a action plan	**12** Try A/B testing
13 Create landing pages	**14** Analize the last two weeks	**15** A/B test landing pages	**16** Do a SEO audit	**17** SEO audit of competitors	**18** Keyword research
19 Improve based on audit	**20** Create keyword content	**21** Create evergreen content	**22** Calculate current conversion rate	**23** Identify problems	**24** Solve blockers
25 Check analytics and funnels	**26** Run SEO Audit	**27** Improve based on audit	**28** Do UX audit	**29** Solve any UX problems	**30** Review 30 day challenge

Set your intention to become a better UX designer and CRO expert with this 30 day callenge! This will make the methods you've learned a bigger part of your everyday work life.

06

More resources for CRO and UX

The last chapter of the book contains more prints of the tools you have encountered in this workbook, so you can use them in future projects!

Resource List

This list will make your life easier

01 Conversion Rate Optimization: A 10 Step-by-Step Guide to Boosting Conversions

Read Now

02 10 tools for UX design to Make Your Life as a Designer Easier

Read Now

03 Personalization Has Not Delivered on Its Promise: 4 ways to fix it

Read Now

04 User Research: A Comprehensive Guide to Understanding Customers and Making Better UX Decisions

Read Now

05 The Five Principles of UX Design Psychology: Can You Predict the Behavior of Your Users?

Read Now

CRO Project Goals

Date:

Goals & Outcomes

Steps to Take

To-Do List

- [ ]
- [ ]
- [ ]
- [ ]
- [ ]

- [ ]
- [ ]
- [ ]
- [ ]
- [ ]

Project Notes

CRO Project Goals

Date:

Goals & Outcomes

Steps to Take

To-Do List

- [ ]
- [ ]
- [ ]
- [ ]
- [ ]

- [ ]
- [ ]
- [ ]
- [ ]
- [ ]

Project Notes

CRO Project Goals

Date:

Goals & Outcomes

Steps to Take

To-Do List

- [ ]
- [ ]
- [ ]
- [ ]
- [ ]

- [ ]
- [ ]
- [ ]
- [ ]
- [ ]

Project Notes

CRO Project Goals

Date:

Goals & Outcomes

Steps to Take

To-Do List

- [ ]
- [ ]
- [ ]
- [ ]
- [ ]

- [ ]
- [ ]
- [ ]
- [ ]
- [ ]

Project Notes

CRO Project Goals

Date:

Goals & Outcomes

Steps to Take

To-Do List

- [ ]
- [ ]
- [ ]
- [ ]
- [ ]

- [ ]
- [ ]
- [ ]
- [ ]
- [ ]

Project Notes